Bossy the Bunny
The Birthday

Pamela Griffiths

First Published 2018

Book 2

Bossy the Bunny

The Birthday

ISBN-10: 1986571602
ISBN-13: 978-1986571609

Classification: Children's Rhyming Story

Website pamelagriffiths.com
Twitter @pamg50
Facebook Author Pamela Griffiths page

Bossy the bunny
At Easter

Book 1 in the bossy the bunny series

Five star review on amazon.co.uk

Bossy the Bunny
The Birthday

Bossy the bunny was happy

His friends have gathered around

The birds flew high above them

Making a chirping sound

Bossy loved to jump and play

Surrounded by his friends

'What can we do today?'

'Well that all depends'

Bossy left them all playing

He had something he must do

He had to make a present

In fact he had to make a few

His brother had a birthday

His two sister's had theirs too

They were all born on the same day

So he planned what he must do

A party was arranged

He made a carrot cake

For the presents he had decided

Some daisy chains he'd make

The birthday was next week

Bossy did the preparations

He had already made a start

On the party decorations

He hid his precious things

Inside a hollow in a tree

They were hidden very well

So that nobody would see

His brother and his sisters

Were completely unaware

They had no idea

That Bossy had a lair

Bossy would surprise them

When their birthday arrived

They were very lucky

They had all survived

Bossy had now realised

His birthday was on the same day

It didn't really matter

He'd enjoy it anyway

The birds were still singing

The sun was shining through

Bossy the bunny thought

'I love my life I do'

Bossy was very busy

There was still so much to do

He asked a few close friends

If they could help him too

His friends said they would help him

They said they wouldn't tell

They made some decorations

And daisy chains as well

The day was fast approaching

The bunnies worked fast and hard

They even took the time

To make a big birthday card

Bossy was so proud of them

His friends were loyal and true

With Bossy the bunny as their leader

There was nothing they wouldn't do

Bossy took all the presents

To a clearing in the wood

They had hidden everything

As best as they could

The party would be held

In just a few more days

Bossy's friends had helped

In so many different ways

They would hang the decorations

At the very last minute

Bossy the bunny dug a hole

And put the decorations in it

'Thank you all my dear friends'

Bossy said 'We're almost done'

'Tomorrow is the birthday

'Then we can all have fun'

'We're glad that we could help'

Bossy's friends replied

They hopped and jumped around

Together side by side

The night before the birthday

There was magic in the air

Excited little bunnies

Were dancing everywhere

Bossy slipped away from them

There were things still to be done

He put the decorations up

All ready for the birthday fun

Bossy's friends had gathered

They had made him a surprise

It was Bossy's birthday too

All beginning at sunrise

Bossy told his family

He wished them 'Happy birthday'

Bossy's brother and his sisters

Were all soon whisked away

Bossy led them into the woods

And gave them a present each

They all had daisy chain garlands

Along with a nice juicy peach

Everyone was happy

'Thank you all' his brother said

'Thank you Bossy' said his sisters

'We've made something for your head'

His sisters gave bossy the bunny

A garland that they had made

'Happy birthday Bossy' they told him

Bossy thanked them and then they played

Bossy the bunny had been surprised

They had all had a very good day

    The birthday had gone very well

    'Now it's time to tidy away'

The birthday had been special

They had all had lots of fun

Now it was all over

With the setting of the sun

Happy birthday

The End

Dedication

For my partner Sandy Hoffman
And my family and friends

For the children who have enjoyed this
story and the adults who have enjoyed reading
this book to them.

Thank you

Pamela Griffiths

For more information about Sheffield author
Pamela Griffiths
(National Award winning poet and author)

Please check out these sites.

Website www.pamelagriffiths.com

Twitter (@pamg56) https://twitter.com/Pamg56

Facebook Author page
https://m.facebook.com/Author-Pamela-Griffiths-167707173288865/

Amazon.co.uk
https://www.amazon.co.uk/Pamela-Griffiths/e/B0034ODJVQ/ref=ntt_dp_epwbk_0